INSPIRATIONAL QUOTES

FROM THE BOOK:
The Quest For God's Love
BY ERIC CHIFUNDA

Eric Chifunda
Cover art by Eric Chifunda

Acknowledgments

My eternal heartfelt gratitude to Harold Klemp, my teacher, my friend, who has inspired me beyond measure.

A special word of thanks to Sean Senatore, publication consultant at Fulton Books Inc. for encouraging me to add more quotes to the book.

I would be remiss not to thank Kristy Bilski at Fulton Books Inc. for her patience during the process of publishing my books.

Through life experiences, we learn what is right and wrong. So choose your actions, thoughts, and plans wisely for they shape your tomorrow and what life gives you back in return and ultimately what you become.

In looking deeper into the play of life, you come to realize that nothing is ever lost, nothing is ever a waste, for life's lessons come from both bad and good circumstances. We are credited for the good and debited for the bad we do. Thus, we suffer for our indiscretions, our bad choices. Conversely, we create better conditions for ourselves by making better choices, taking the middle road, being kind to the weak, being there for others in their hour of need, helping out in coin as needed and as able. Such selfless acts make for a better and more fulfilling life.

Those attuned to the needs of others
are often a blessing and a light to those
in need. They become messengers
of love who enliven not only their
lives, but also those they serve.

Life provides us with endless opportunities for spiritual advancement. As you grow in your awareness, you will note that there's a spiritual gem embedded in each activity. If you can recognize that, you are increasingly living in the consciousness of Divine Spirit.

To know who we are, to reclaim our true nature, we must let go of our superficial identity, revise our wrong thought processes, recant our outmoded erroneous old beliefs of who we are and in doing so, we will begin to chart a new course. We will start to awaken to our true nature—Soul.

For the most part, our behavior is supposed reflect what we are as loving Souls. But the pressures of daily lives make us forget our true identity as Soul, thus we tend to often lose our spiritual bearings. To regain our spiritual footing, we need to slow down a little, contemplate upon the permanency of our true identity as Soul. Once we begin to delve within ourselves, in the quietude of the moment, we will gradually start to re-awaken to our higher Soul self.

Each one of us has our God given mission.
Once we recognize it and begin to work
toward achieving it, this becomes a
gift to the world designed to uplift.

છ૭

In your endeavor to become a willing
instrument of God, God be with you
as your daily protector, comforter,
guide, and teacher on your journey
toward God's dream for you.

We tend to focus on change that takes place on the outer and pay little attention to the inner. The truth of the matter is that real change of lasting value often takes place on the inner. Hence it's good to pay attention to night dreams. However inner change revealed through dreams needs to be approached and carefully interpreted because it can be open to a wide range of misinterpretations.

Everybody is Soul, yet not many know
who they truly are. Love is the key
element that begins to open the window
to the qualities of the inner Soul self.
Love is the key that allows the ego self
to yield to the higher Soul Self.

cs

And it is this awakening to Soul Self that
leads to the gradual understanding of who
we are as conscious children of God.

The Godliness you become a part of is the measure of the love you can give out to the world through selfless acts. Love itself is God in action. For all things done out of love, with love, for love are godly even though their outer appearance is deceptively mundane.

☙

So to understand God's love and express it in its true essence, one must awaken one's inner consciousness and learn to embrace God within.

We exist to discover the power of love. If we can travel this path that can lead us to the discovery of more love in its pure and higher form, our lives will likewise improve in proportion to how much love we can embrace and give out. For it's in accepting this love that we undergo a transformation. It is in giving it back to life that we grow in our capacity for more love.

It is love, that inner God impulse, that moves you to act out of selflessness. It is love that sustains you through periods of turmoil, apparent failure, setbacks, and discouragements.

An action born out of love is enduring. It transcends the physical act in its quality and impact. Love, if allowed to be the force behind any action has lasting power and influence on all that it touches. It is this type of love coupled with courage that moves people, communities, and nations to a higher level and to move forward.

It is love that drives you to help others in need. It's this type of love that is fair, kind, considerate, yet firm in its course in bringing about positive changes. It is love that drives you to live in higher planes of consciousness while here on earth. So that though you are in this world, you are indeed not of this world. Because with love in your heart, your heart lives in the heavens while lending support to your outer life and actions.

When there's truth in what we do or say, done out of honesty and necessity with intent to do well for the greater good, all will be well in the end. Sometimes the immediate effect may not be comfortable, because we are not always comfortable with the truth. Because truth makes us come face to face with ourselves, our shortcomings, our human frailties.

One way to come into a close relationship
with Divine Spirit is to let go of all
materiality that holds us in bondage
to this world. In so doing, we allow
control of your outer life through self-
will to be guided by Divine Spirit.

Once the problem of ego-self is understood spiritually, life as we know it changes. It does not change in the way it runs or unfolds, but changes in the way you view it. And as you change the way you view life, you naturally change the way you live your life. With this newly acquired ability, you are now able to see more clearly, beyond illusion.

Everything is contingent upon our perception of ourselves. The more we have a positive outlook of ourselves and that of others, the more others will see us in a positive light. So let's examine ourselves and determine what attitudes need to be changed and matched with our new, higher values so our relationship with life can be more positive.

Patience is an essential factor that can go a long way in helping us move steadily toward reaching our goal. It is helpful to realize the importance of cultivating the virtue of patience in all things we do. Lack of it can cause one to rush and easily stumble and fall. It is when we rush that we make the most mistakes.

When pure love dawns, thoughts of the beloved evoke warm feelings of love and joy. What is it that causes such positive feelings? Is it an anticipation of something good to happen? Once you have this experience, you want to capture it again and again. It's never a selfish emotion. It's never love that is imposing. It is the type that makes one feel serene and joyful within one's inner being.

We are where we are because we have accepted this reality as is. To go beyond where we are now, we need to start letting go of our current limiting thoughts. We need to awaken to the fact that our thinking and expectations, are limited to what we see and believe. If we let go, let the Divine Spirit guide us to where It needs us, the hold we have imposed unknowingly or knowingly on ourselves will be lessened or be removed. And the Divine Spirit will have the most profound influence and the power to take us beyond. Beyond into the inner unseen God worlds.

Since God is the creator, He has the power to recreate your life if you let Him. To let Him, you must submit and surrender to Him. It is surrender that opens the human gate to allow re-entry of Divine Spirit. For one to maintain this state of conscious union with Divine Spirit, surrender is the key for it yields a deeper connection with Divine Spirit. And it is in this deeper connection that you live your life fully.

Without love, you have nothing. Thus, it behooves you to go out and surrender yourself to love. In surrendering, you will experience love in a way that no one else does because it brings out a unique individuality in you as no two people are ever alike. It's this uniqueness that touches people that will set you apart from others. That is what happens when you come from a place of love in what you say, do, and think.

Disorganization is costly in terms of time and money. It can cost you missed deadlines, missed opportunities, missed due bill payments. The disorder is the root of a life that is misdirected, wasteful, chaotic, and muddled. In this state, priorities get misdirected. Once order is re-instituted, life becomes a joy to live again. Things become easily accessible, and work becomes more efficient, life becomes easier to handle, to run, to live again. One can breathe again with relief, and have peace of mind amid order. With an organized life, one can now stop and enjoy life a little more easily as things will now run a little bit more smoothly.

To have love in one's life at a conscious level daily is to live a life of love, governed by love, sustained by love, blessed by the magic power of love. Look to your heart to understand the real language of love. Its language is truth. Its language aims at awakening you to its ways that are so many, so subtle yet so commonplace that we overlook them.

Give back to life what you have gained from life and God. Give back to life what God gave you. And that gift is the gift of love packaged according to each person's makeup, consciousness, and calling.

A detached life is a life lived in freedom from the shackles of this world. Freedom to stand on your own feet with complete reliance on Divine Spirit for guidance and protection yet remain fully engaged in your daily life.

Love is universal, yet it's personal for it manifests through you as its operating distributor. To be a good love distributor one ought to learn its ways, its philosophy, its power, its reality. How it manifests at the human level vs global level.

જી

If you open your heart, love will show you its ways and how to give it, when to give it, and how much of it to give out.

One feature about expanded consciousness is that it speeds up one's pace in life because one can now live a life of greater responsibility and can handle more on account of newly attained spiritual strength. Your circle of experience expands in proportion to the degree that your inner world has grown as you make corresponding adjustments in the outer. Before this expansion, you may only have had a few friends, interests, choices, but because of your expanded consciousness, you may have an expansion in different aspects of your life, as needed, for you will have gained greater freedom, strength, wisdom and love. Your world will become bigger, richer and more dynamic. Your love for life will increase in strength and depth.

To regain our spiritual footing, we need to slow down a little, contemplate upon the permanency of our identity as Soul. Once we begin to delve within ourselves, in the quietude of the moment, we will gradually start to awaken to our higher Soul self.

We must resist engaging in negative elements that taint Soul and work to consistently be ethical in order to remain in that Soul state. It's a state of love, balance, happiness, moderation, patience, wisdom, freedom, love, and strength. It is by staying in the positive state that we reclaim what we are as loving Souls

With faculties of Soul, you can transcend the limits of human consciousness and tap into the God power. To know God the way you do in your way at your level of acceptance takes engagement of Soul senses.

We can know that love exists
everywhere only if our hearts, eyes,
and ears are open enough to feel,
see, receive, give, and experience that
true love leaves no room for fear.

When you have love, life presents itself in a new light. When you have love, God presents Himself in a way that you become aware of its guiding presence. It is love that makes God become the predominant influence in your life. And as God becomes the essence and basis of your life, your actions serve to make life better. Thus you must follow God with every fiber of your being. God will, in turn, embrace you, protect you, infuse you with His infinite wisdom, freedom, power, and love.

Loving God can be easy yet difficult for those held in bondage to this material world. Difficult for those who consider intellectualism as superior to love. Difficult for those afflicted by their poverty in materiality. Difficult for those who are dominated by their riches. The key to loving God is in one's ability to recognize that in loving, your life becomes a joy it is meant to be. Loving God starts with loving people close to you. That is the starting point.

Trust is the keyword that opens the door so that love can enter. Trust that all will go well according to Divine Will. Trust that things will be taken care of while you do your part at the human level. Keep in mind that loving God and letting Him work through you is the key to living a full life.

The voice of God is the inner voice that guides us in the right way. Once the voice speaks, it is spiritual truth. Once you hear it, follow it with determination and steadfastness. It is a way of God. It is a journey beckoning you to follow God. It is not always easy because it takes us where the routinized mind can't go. To places not always familiar, but always right. Not always easy, but always right. Not always logical, but always right. Not always what we expect, but always right. That is just the way of God: not always our way.

God loves you in ways you will never fully understand. God remains linked to you through love. Love is a line of communication that God uses to stay connected with you. Love is the only way God serves and sustains all His creation. Love is what keeps us nourished spiritually. Love, therefore, is Soul food without which Soul can't do.

To love yourself is the first step in recognizing GOD's love for you. If you don't love yourself, it's difficult to love God. If you hate yourself it is difficult to love anything outside yourself. You can only give out what you have within you. If you have hatred, that's what you will give out consciously or unconsciously. Love changes everything.

Being love by nature, you ought to act to reveal your real primary quality-love.

❧

Love should be the mainstay of your actions. Love should be the prime mover in all you do, all you think, and all you feel.

❧

God loves His creations, so it behooves you to be humble enough, patient enough, spiritually awake enough, to recognize and appreciate God's love in whatever form it comes to you. Open your spiritual eyes and ears so as to recognize and acknowledge your Divine place in its all- encompassing, all-loving, all-inclusive, limitless consciousness.

It helps to listen to the voice of love in all things that come into your life since all life has at its epicenter the essence of love. You will see it if you keep your heart open. For only love in your heart can see love in other things. And the degree to which you realize love in yourself is the same degree to which you will recognize it in others.

The act of putting love in all we do yields a secondary yet more essential effect: It steers us in the right direction in our journey home to God. Each action imbued and driven by love brings us closer to our true nature. Our true nature is a happy and loving Soul. In embracing our true nature, we are embracing God, in actuality the spirit of God. It is through this reciprocal action that our marriage with Divine Spirit becomes one with each other.

In giving back to life without expecting
anything in return, you are giving a gift
that keeps on giving. A gift that enriches
in more ways than one. In ways in
which an invisible connection of unity
gets established between the sender
and recipient. This makes for a better
relationship with those we love and serve.

You learn to grow in awareness at each stage of each goal attained. Soul, in the process, learns how to survive on earth, progressively, in dimension and self-awareness, which leads to spiritual freedom. Freedom to soar above the entrapments of this world. You, as Soul, have now gained wisdom on what it takes to survive here on earth.

ॐ

If you can't make it here, how do you expect to make it in the inner higher worlds commonly called heavens? So start here and become a success here before you can expect to succeed in the unseen God worlds beyond.

When you give something without
expecting anything in return, you allow
God to determine the course of its effect.
But when you give something and expect
something back, you are imposing human
limitations in it, which limits how far
our actions can affect what we do, the
nature and character of the effect. So if
you want to have maximum positive effect
on your actions, step back and let God
be in charge of the effects of your actions.
This kind of attitude yields not only
greater love and trust for God, but also
a greater bond between you and God.

Love in its pure form, in its divine
form, lights up the dark alleys of
our lives, opens up our inner eyes to
enable us to view life more clearly.

When we start a task and leave it unfinished, the flow of Divine Spirit, which was giving sustenance to that act is suspended as long as we don't resume that activity.

℘

So learn to finish things once started unless Divine Spirit steers you in another direction.

The connection people make with God is a personal one. Therefore the journey to God is always their own even if people belong to the same path, or religion. So it is incumbent upon each person to determine for themselves what path fits them, what resonates with them.

Forcing another into your religion is a violation of that person's right and freedom of choice of religion or path. Unless you know the person's spiritual needs, able to walk in their shoes, you are not in the position to choose what path is best for them spiritually.

It is in living in the now that you become re-aligned with life. It is in being in the moment that you re-establish the direct link with God. It is in being present with God in the now that God becomes your daily companion.

It is love from which other laws stem. The inner personal commandments are written in the spirit of love. Love as it applies to your individuality limited in its outer expression by your capacity and attitude. Its external form is shaped and expressed through our limited human consciousness. This pure love, in its real spiritual form is limitless and its source inexhaustible.

We can tap into this source
via obedience to God

To live in obedience to Divine Spirit's guidance is to succeed in living a life of spirit truly. There's no greater success, in essence, than spiritual enlightenment. So live it, become it, and embrace it and all else will fall into place.

Soul is the real innermost makeup of you. It is indestructible, and has capacity to love because in essence it is made from the same loving cloth of God. It inhabits aspects of God with which it was made. Realizing these God aspects leads to a greater understanding and better relationship with life and God.

❧

And when you, its child, awakens to your true heritage, God rejoices.

By giving love from the position of Soul, you will learn to love the highest in your friends, family, and those you meet irrespective of what and who they are.

People in different paths have their own spiritual guides they look to for upliftment for there are many ways to connect with God that will fit individuals at different levels of consciousness all over the world. Therefore, there cannot be only one way as God is not limited to one select group of people. In the human state we tend to limit God to what group He favors or belongs to. The truth of the matter is that God created all living things, therefore He belongs to all. So within this vast limitless realm of God, each person has the free will to choose a path that best fits that individual.

You must take action where you need to. But don't let your actions be dictated by fear. Use love as your guiding principle. With love, you can spiritually conquer anything. It's good to remember that, with a loving attitude, you can open others hearts. And with an open heart, God can work through you. Armed with God's light, you can bring light to others. And their walls of illusion and resistance they built through ignorance may begin to break down. Nothing can help them save God.

Always look to God to avoid as well as enable you to overcome unnecessary traps, uncalled for inconveniences that often come through your ignorance and stubbornness. God, if allowed to work through you, He will bring wonders into your life. You need to just learn to trust Him, give of yourself to Him, align your actions with the guidance you receive that you believe and understand is from God. By so doing, you will be aligning your will with God's will.

One way God communicates with us is through Sound. Sound manifests itself as sounds of nature as well as human voice in the outer world we live in. Some sounds are audible and others are inaudible. The outer sounds are echos of the inner sounds that issue from Godhead. Hearing them at a deeper level with inner ears can open one to Divine Spirit. This process of opening yields spiritual purification. It purifies, uplifts whoever has the good fortune, training, purity, and self-discipline to hear it. It is the music of God coming to bless you. Coming to uplift you and free you from the conditions that are holding you down in the meshes of human consciousness and its strong superficial identity with materiality.

For those who wish to hear these inner sounds, they can try out spiritual exercises taught in ECKANKAR, the Path of Spiritual Freedom. They are not designed to change your spiritual belief or religion, but if anything, to deepen your connection with Divine Spirit. They are universal and have spiritually liberating effect on anyone who diligently practices them. To do them is a privilege for they will transform you spiritually. Making you a more spiritually awakened person than you were before. When you hear God speak through His voice as Sound, you are blessed beyond words, beyond compare, beyond your wildest imagination.

With love, things reorganize themselves to a new order to allow for more love to flow. That is why the way of love is the way to heaven on earth. Heaven on earth predicated on the state of consciousness we operate from. We are the ones who determine our heaven by our inner state.

Life can be viewed as comprising of innumerable rooms, each with its own experiences designed to strengthen us spiritually. These experiences gradually yield wisdom, freedom, and love. There's no end to growing in our capacity for more love. There's always another key to be earned for entry into another room, always a larger room. And each successive room comes with its own gifts, obstacles, lessons, all designed to make us stronger and better. It's upto us to walk through the door to get all the gifts we need that pertain to that room during that time period.

If we fulfill the conditions needed to move to the next room, larger room, we will have grown measurably in our capacity for more love. With more love so gained, we can move to new experiences as we journey on home to God.

To love with an open heart is to embrace and attract life in its fullness. To love with this open heart is the key to serving life selflessly. When you serve life in this way, you are becoming love as love becomes you.

Learn to step back and look at life events closely and watch the play of spirit. The recognition of the Divine spirit at work is a function of an honest and steadfast engagement of your spiritual faculties of sight and hearing. The more you use them, the more acute your spiritual senses become. The increased clarity enables you to see God's actions more clearly, day by day, minute by minute, when necessary.

Soul is often overlooked because it lies hidden behind covers of the physical embodiment. Thus it behooves us to love the manifestations of God in whatever form they appear. And if we don't like the form, we should at least go past that form to Soul. In doing so, it makes it easier to love another as Soul despite the physical barriers. We should awaken to the fact that all things around us have God's essence in them despite their outer imperfections. Besides, nothing is perfect in this world.

❧

In looking beyond the physical imperfections, we'll recognize that God's love is all around us. We will then live our lives, knowing that it's God that gives us love through the gift of life all around us.

When God gives you love, He knows what you need and how you can receive it. God gives only in proportion to what you can receive and handle. God gives only when you are ready in your consciousness. When you are too expectant, you may not receive God's gift because you are too tensed. When you are relaxed and not expecting anything, you may receive the gift because it's in the relaxed state that we stay open to receiving.

It is only in loving others, being open
to life, and new experiences that we
grow in our capacity for more love. Love
God through loving life for love is the
common denominator in all living things.
In loving life and God's creatures, you
will realize that love and God are one.

Love will show us how to love if only we can be humble enough to listen to the voice of life. Our sincere desire for truth, to live by the code of truth, will always lead one to truth, higher truth, which in itself reveals the presence of greater love. Love and truth co-exist to build on each other. So that when you love truth, this love becomes the key that opens the door to the discovery of higher spiritual truth, which in turn yields greater love.

When you have love, it propels you to higher spiritual heights, beyond the reach of human consciousness. Because love is the only building block that has the power to catapult us to Godhead. Love nourishes what you start and follow through. Love lends strength and sustains what you set out to achieve if you stay focused. Go for love, and the entire world will move with you if not follow you. For love, uplifts and the universe tends toward moving up and forward.

Love, in its Divine form, has the power
to transform one to an awakened spiritual
individual, who will pulsate with love,
and get connected to the essence of God.
With pure love, one walks this earth while
the heart lives in the joyous heavenly state
with God above, making one an integrated
spiritual human whole imbued with love,
blessed by love, embraced by love and guided
by love. Learn to cultivate this Divine love,
and your life shall be lifted beyond measure.

We never get away from what we set in motion. The more of the actions we engage in, the more of a variety of experiences we have, the more of a variety of spiritual lessons we set ourselves up to learn. The less we do, the less we learn from life.

Actions driven by love activate the dormant love lying within the depth of our hearts. Once activated, share it, give it out where needed. Be practical and commonsensical about it in order to make it a daily active and helpful part of you. It's by doing daily selfless deeds for which you expect no repayment that you genuinely live this love.

Once the little self is brought under control, the higher self that operates under a different and higher law takes over. Love begins to pour out to the appropriate open, ready, and willing recipients around you, near and far, invisible and visible. Just be careful how you give it: Avoid placing limiting conditions on it—ensure it is selfless. Don't take credit for the dividends that come your way.

ℰℐ

They are love's way of rewarding your selfless acts of love.

God knows our life cycles, our right partner, our right job, our proper diet at any given time. It will bring into our being and our reach all things at the right time that are beneficial to us. The challenge is in how to figure out and recognize the guidance when it comes.

All we can do is trust implicitly and surrender to God our cares, concerns, fears, limitations, and in return we get what we need spiritually in the right proportion, at the right time, and on God's terms.

By giving of yourself to life where and when needed, and when able, you will begin to tap into the God power. The nature of this power is to serve life.

❧

So if you love God above all else, you will want to serve life selflessly. With that, you will become an integral part of life and become its loyal servant, not in a slavish, blind way, but in a very conscious, willing, and loving way.

Look to God and say a prayer of gratitude. For all that represents freedom and independence, has in some way, been touched by the hand of God, so that the freedom we enjoy now is, to a great extent, the freedom bestowed on us from God through human effort, struggle, and sacrifice.

When God is in charge, life gets turned around. Life becomes rearranged in a new and better order. Rearranged such that a higher order emerges. When this happens, learn to keep it going. Keep it going in a forward direction. It's an exciting and enjoyable ride. But you must be courageous enough to ride it. It's a ride of God. Hang on and keep up, or if you resist, you will be dragged along unwillingly, causing you to endure unnecessary suffering.

Learn to channel your love to accomplish more productive service in whatever form possible. Be active, be loving, and be giving. But give your love wisely, selectively where and when needed in this world.

When we awaken our inner consciousness, and look back, we will find that we are no longer the same person who started. By gaining spiritual answers through listening to the inner guidance, we become spiritually transformed into a new being with expanded consciousness. We become a living and walking example of what it means to realize the truth. Once we learn how to hear and follow the voice of God, we begin to walk a direct path to God.

ဢ

And no one can walk the path of truth for us save ourselves.

Open your heart and let love in, it's not intended for you to hoard it and hide it in your heart, but to pass it on to those who need it. To do so, you must let love guide you as to who merits it and in what way to share it. So that whatever you do, whatever you think, whatever you plan at its core, there is love as a guiding principle.

So let in God's love. This essence of God will enter your heart, purify it, and with the power of love, reach all within your orbit of experience and grace them with its presence.

એ

On account of that, you will become a joy to those who know you as you leave them a little happier, a little better, and a little more loved than before.

What you are as Soul is shown in various aspects of your unique way of expressing God's love through your actions, your innate abilities, gifts, skills, and many other ways through which Soul expresses itself through love in this world. Engaging in such is the beginning of self-recognition of what you are as Soul. The innermost loving part of ourselves God loves and with which He is concerned.

❦

Your participation in what you love becomes a window through which God makes His presence known in your life.

When you hoard love, it fills up your cup and overflows, your life may spiral out of control, out of balance, because you close the channel on the outgoing end. To regain balance between the inflow and outflow of love from God at the outgoing end, you need to pass love to others, to life, to the universe where it belongs- to serve a purpose. Keep in mind that love is purposeful.

By loving those who are close to you, your heart easily begins to open because there is less resistance, and there is the element of implied trust. When your heart opens, then you can start making steps toward loving God, because the prerequisite to loving God is an open heart. It's an open heart that has the capacity to discern and embrace God's love.

Beyond this world of appearances exists a world that is real but operates at a higher level of vibrations beyond the range of perception of human vision. To see beyond, one ought to employ spiritual senses that are adaptive to the higher vibrations of the unseen world. Getting a glimpse of the hidden world changes one's outlook on life. One begins to view life a little more clearly. One understands a bit better the relative reality we live in, fear of death goes away, for one now knows that life continues beyond this world.

Let us change gears by turning on a new leaf, and wasting no more time. If we plan our days and nights well, there will be enough time to fulfill our goals and some time left for leisure as well. Time well planned is time well invested and enjoyed.

Each one of us has a God-given mission. Once we recognize it and work toward achieving it, this becomes a gift to the world designed to uplift.

To spiritualize yourself, you can pray, meditate, contemplate or chant HU (pronounced as HUE), an ancient charged love sound that can uplift, purify you, and open your heart to Divine love, regardless of your religion or belief. You can sing this word silently or aloud daily ten to fifteen minutes or anytime you are facing adversity, anxiety, or stressed. Learn to listen with your heart and act from the higher ground within you. Such is a way to live from the spiritual state within you. And from this vantage point, your life will become a joy to live.

Divine Spirit operates in such a way it moves life forward. It is dynamic and responsive to our individual needs that are in keeping with its nature. Thus it will guide one once engaged in whatever you do that is uplifting.

If you understand and apply the basic principle of surrender to the Divine Spirit, your life can be put in order again. Yes, you can have your life re-ordered by Divine Spirit. All you need to do is trust and surrender to Its impeccable guidance. And it will elevate you to greatest heights. For it is in seeking the highest that the rest of our life falls into place.

We need patience in order to achieve anything of worth. Absolute patience is a virtue we must all learn by which to live. With patience, we safeguard ourselves against premature quitting as we endeavor to pursue our goals. We have to learn to hang on despite discouragements and setbacks along the way. With such steadfast, disciplined attitude, we can reach any goal of worth.

Our real home is the heavens, far beyond the lower heavens, right into the pure God worlds, to the very hallowed home of God. So our purpose is indeed a noble one despite our humble outer conditions. And that is to live an uplifting life, with the conscious knowingness that we are God's children, and for that, we are eternally blessed and grateful.

One who cares about what they do, often wants to ensure that what they do is done well. When something is done well, no matter how small the activity might be, it has the power to touch other people in a way that evokes and inspires love in their hearts. Such an act has a hand of God in it and will have their hearts filled with love.

❦

So do well, finish what you start, and your life will be ever more enriching in measures beyond your expectations.

Act with a conscious effort to tune in to the needs of the moment. In other words, learn not to rush through life, for love never rushes. Do all in love's time. When we make missteps, realize that they are there to awaken us to greater love as we learn how to avoid a repetition of such violation. Mistakes and failures along the way are part of the cosmic plan to teach us how to align ourselves with the law of love. Violating the law of love, repeating the same mistakes over and over again serves to set us up for a life of unnecessary suffering brought on by our unbending will not to do the right thing.

&

It's through acts of love, consideration, and fairness that our life becomes enriched, blessed with good fortune that gives us a great sense of well-being.

Often we are unaware of what our real spiritual needs are because our sight is not clear. Our sight is oftentimes clouded by our emotions and unconscious or willful ignorance. Emotions clouded in chains of attachment to old loves, outmoded values, old habits, and fears, falsely believing that things should always remain the same as they have ever been. False peace, comfort zone, and familiarity trap us.

Do everything with the belief and knowledge that God's love is in action, in our thoughts and feelings. Have no concern for any negativity but recognize it for what it is and deal with it accordingly for in it are lessons of love. So, look at apparent negativity as blessings in disguise. Stay focused on doing all in God's name, and your life will run a little more smoothly.

It is in living life in fullness that God supports you in fullness because God helps those who help themselves. So remember to embrace life so life can return its embrace. Once you embrace life with love, life must support you, for God always returns the favor a hundredfold.

The journey into the mystery of life is
endless and can be complex, therefore, it
takes great care to correctly fathom it at
different levels, both deep and superficial.

Why doesn't God give us easy answers? Could it be that the answers are clear except our hearing and sight are faulty? Could it be that Divine Spirit is trying to guide us in the right direction, but we are not aware, or we refuse to follow? Could it be that we hold onto old ways tenaciously that we resist right and new ways that may come about? Could it be that we have not purified our hearts enough to hear the guiding voice of God? Could it be that God is always present with us, but we are not still available to God through our ignorance, pride, or stubbornness?

Like attracts like. Similarly, love attracts love. So all things love will be drawn to you equivalent to how much love you give. Give only in the spirit of love so that you create an environment in which others come to share their love.

On your life journey home to God, should you feel tired, rest if you must, and should you fall as it may happen innumerable times, by God pick yourself up and trudge along. It is in getting back up that we awaken to greater realization, if only for a moment, of our divinity and eternal nature as Soul.

To help others learn to stand on their feet, don't do for them what they can do for themselves. If you were to do so, you would be playing an unintended retrogressive role in that person's life. It would help if you gave of yourself when there is a real need to uplift another, bring a measure of comfort, provide needed help, a shoulder to lean on, or institute a change in society for the good of all.

There's great wisdom in taking one's time to learn well lessons embedded in life's challenges and changes. For with patience, the dust will eventually settle, rendering things clearer. In the moment of clarity, you will regain your footing and enjoy the good fruits born of change.

It is essential to recognize that words, deeds, thoughts fueled and executed with anger are always destructive. The problem is that as these actions born out of anger begin to come back as adverse effects, we don't recognize their origin. Thus we are often unable to link them to our past actions. Unfortunately, we begin to point fingers, blaming everyone but ourselves. Blinded by our emotions and unable to see the causal link, we repeat the same cycle, making the same mistakes over and over and continue to suffer the effects emanating from our negative thoughts and deeds.

What is the right way to work with the Divine Spirit? The right way is to let Divine Spirit use us. We adjust our lives, so we do everything according to Divine Will. But often in our effort to harmonize our will with Divine will, we err by trying to bend and reduce this higher will to conform to our terms, which often are selfish. A first step in the right direction is to learn to listen to the voice of God without predetermining the outcome, resisting to listen to the self-righteous and egotistical voice of the mind. This way, we steer clear of the psychic entrapments and mind stuff.

The journey into the mystery of life is
endless and can be complex, therefore, it
takes great care to correctly fathom it at
different levels, both deep and superficial.

Why doesn't God give us easy answers?
Could it be that the answers are clear except
our hearing and sight are faulty? Could
it be that Divine Spirit is trying to guide
us in the right direction, but we are not
aware, or we refuse to follow? Could it be
that we hold onto old ways tenaciously
that we resist right and new ways that
may come about? Could it be that we
have not purified our hearts enough to
hear the guiding voice of God? Could it
be that God is always present with us, but
we are not still available to God through
our ignorance, pride, or stubbornness?

Being grateful prepares our hearts to receiving more of life's gifts. Answers come more easily to the one with a grateful heart. That is so because a grateful heart is an open heart. And an open heart is a receptive heart. A receptive heart is a heart of Gold. A heart of Gold is a loving heart. A loving heart has a direct link to God. And therein lies the secret to getting answers from God

Despite the pains and joys on your life journey, as you expand in consciousness and understanding, you begin to realize that life is intended to lead you to God via love. And the difficulties you face along the way are designed to temper you as Soul, to awaken you to your real nature – a side of you that is indestructible. This realization of your eternal nature will change the way you view life, and consequently how you live your life.

Some people have learned how to listen
to the inner voice of God. The inner
voice, if not listened to, grows fainter
and eventually fades into silence. Some
have the purity of heart to hear the inner
voice of God that continually speaks to
us when we are ready to listen in. Most
of us don't listen to it because we are too
caught up in the outer world of materiality.
So stop for a moment, listen to the inner
voice, so you can begin to open up to
Divine love, and through that, you will
gradually know who you are as Soul.

In the human state, we are concerned
with our image. Thus we put on an
artificial façade to present to the public
that is praiseworthy. It, therefore, takes
the strength of character, courage, grit,
and a great sense of self-honesty to face
ourselves and follow the inner guidance
and carry through with necessary actions.
This requires adopting a risk-taking attitude
that would catapult one above the social
forces of conformity. It is by rising above
all opposing social forces that we muster up
enough courage to answer our own unique
call of Soul -- from God…. This could
lead to significant improvement in our life,
spiritual awareness, and material sufficiency.

With the right motivation, sincerity, self-discipline, hard work, proper, and precise goal setting, we are more likely to be more productive and lead a more fulfilling life. As such, the dividends go beyond monetary benefits. It becomes a life of fulfillment in more ways than one.

To get answers from God, it helps to stay open without expectations of how the answer will come. The attitude of expecting nothing yet expecting whatever Divine Spirit gives us is the best way to open ourselves to recognizing and receiving answers from God when they come.

To live a life of self-responsibility, ensure you live up to what is expected of you in social, business, and spiritual contracts. With such, you will be of service to life more than you would ever imagine. Doing all that we have agreed with others, in some way, is fulfilling God's contracts because God works through our actions, what we do, and how we conduct ourselves.

Through our actions, we bring
God's spirit to bear.

One needs to go beyond the little self to externalize love, to bring it out to the world through some modus operandi, often through one's talent, interest, special ability, love given to another unconditionally.

Divine Love is the only force that can take
one beyond time, space, energy, and matter.

☙

Because of its penetrative nature, it is
the only force that permeates and creates
a common link among all things that
have life. For everything that has life
is sustained in some way by love.

Perhaps one may look to a spiritual guide or God for guidance as to which way to go in our life.

❧

A simple approach could be; God show me thy way, and invoke the well known prayer; Thy Will be done. Thus making ourselves receptive to God's guidance.

❧

With God's hand in it, the change will be met more easily with confidence.

When we perform actions driven by love, they tend to open closed hearts through which love connects with those to whom we give love. But it has to be the right action which acts as a conduit for love. Thus a wrong act can unwittingly lead to less love. So to truly love, you must genuinely act selflessly with love. You do so by giving yourself genuinely to the other person. You must do it unconditionally without expecting anything in return.

The past has an uncanny way of resurfacing. It often resurfaces because we still hold onto specific outmoded and unworthy thoughts in our minds. That means recreating conditions we wish to eliminate. And forgetting that life always moves us forward. Life always gives us new opportunities to explore. Life presents us with new situations to experience in order to afford us a chance to learn and grow.

With enlightenment comes a proper understanding of the harsh realities of this life. With understanding, pains of awareness are assuaged, thus making our day-to-day challenges of life a little easier to handle. Despite our pains of awareness, it is helpful to remember that the harsh realities of life are designed to make us stronger, wiser, and more loving.

When God speaks, we tend to listen with our minds through the filter of logic. But God's message comes from the source beyond the reaches of logic. Hence all we receive is filtered and distorted messages that are forced to conform to logic. When God lights up the way so we can avoid the snares from the negative force, our logical eyes are too limited to see. So we misconstrue the messages coming from up above, thus receive incorrect information, which then guides our lives in the wrong direction, causing us to trip and fall and hurt ourselves. We cry and wonder why God didn't prevent this from happening.

Sometimes God takes away something we may be too attached to that serve as an obstacle to our growth. If we are too attached to that object and have a false dependency on it for our survival, we often resist, fight tooth and nail, refusing to let go out of fear and ignorance. Because letting go could be a blessing in disguise, as this could be a crutch we need to get rid of but we are unable to recognize it for what it is because our inner vision is blind and we are deaf to the ways of God. Yet we wonder why God doesn't help us and give us guidance in the affairs of our life.

Love, at its more profound level, is the God force that is unconditional. But once conditions are imposed on it, its unhindered flow gets blocked commensurate to the type and degree of blockage. A vague echo and tainted love are what become manifest in your life. To avoid this, try to love without conditions, and the world will open its treasures to you. If you love with conditions, the world will deny you its true wealth, the heavenly more superior wealth that you can never put a price on it. So it behooves you to love without conditions, and you will become a living, pulsating, magnet of love.

We are Soul in actuality. But we know not because our vision is blinded by the allures of the material world. Our outward focus renders us blind. Blind to our higher spiritual nature. Blind to our true essence. Blind to our divinity. Blind to our higher reality. Blind to our real mission. But there are few that muster up enough courage, self-honesty, and moral strength to look within for who and what they are.

As you give and receive, you grow in your capacity to store more, receive more, and give more love. Your universe can't help but expand in all aspects of your life. You will be able to touch more Souls. Your role, therefore, is to identify gifts that issue from God designed for you. Once identified, partake in them, and by so doing you are truly serving God and living in the presence of God. So pass on the gifts, don't hoard them in some dark hole. They don't belong in hidden places where no one sees them save you. They belong to the universe. They are there for the enrichment of all, including yourself and others.

Rigid thoughts, beliefs, attitudes, expectations at the mind level serve to block Soul and cater to the mind. To let go of the tight hold on these thoughts, which are often earthbound, opens doors to allow Divine Spirit in. Letting go happens by persuasion, not by force of one's will. It occurs by an implicit trust in Divine Spirit. With this release on one's rigid thought processes, we enter a world of real spiritual, higher action.

Love is what makes life change for the better. The elements of love can sometimes be found in life situations that sometimes appear negative. It takes purity of mind and heart for one to see beyond the illusion of negativity. You see good because you have good within your heart. You recognize love because you view life from the vantage point of your heart. You feel love because your heart is open to love. You love because you embrace and face life with a loving attitude. You enjoy life because you recognize it is a gift from God.

You serve God by living a life filled with love. What that means is that you go about your business with a loving attitude. A loving attitude steeped in love for life, and God, stemming from the discipline from living within the laws of spirit. Meaning, you must listen to Divine Spirit daily and follow Its dictates as much as is practical. In other words, Divine Spirit begins to dictate your life in a way that benefits you immensely, for it can't work against its nature but make your life more expansive and abundant.

When you put love in everything you do,
love comes back to you a hundredfold.
Love, the only element that will sustain you
without diminishing if given from the heart.

༄

In love, there's truth. And in truth
lies strength. Strength becomes the
backbone upon which love grows.

The power of love is the greatest power ever if coupled with courage. Greatness is a mark of truth, strength, and courage to do what seems humanly impossible, which takes implicit faith in the magical power of love. Love without faith and trust will sooner or later make your effort falter, and what you set out to accomplish may not come to full fruition.

౭ఌ

Faith opens the flow of the power of love. An unshakeable belief in the power of love can create a pathway for love to come through to help you climb the heights to spiritual greatness.

If God's power is allowed to willingly and freely work through us, we will accomplish great works never before imagined. Because God's power knows no limits, and human laws do not bind it. So to serve life effectively, one needs to humble oneself before God and ask with sincerity the best way to serve life with gifts one has. One will be guided to the right contacts, places, situations, where one can serve with love in the best way possible. All one needs to do is to ask honestly, and the answer will come in some way, sooner or later. And when the response is received, and it feels spiritually right, by God, do all you can to make this a reality. Put your heart into it. Keep in mind that you are doing this not for self but for the greater good.

It is when something is done to gain others recognition that we fall into a negative trap. To serve life honestly and selflessly, fully to the best of our ability, we need to be the best we can be and do the best in the name of God.

With deeper insight, with a mind uncluttered, freed of doubts, fears, anxieties, we would gain an in-depth knowingness beyond doubts, beyond limits of our minds what blessings are coming to us. With that, our lives would become a little more forgiving, showing the power of the gift of insight into life's blessings that make life easier and more enjoyable each day.

In love is truth is at its core. Fear implies the presence of untruth. Therefore a search for truth is, in effect, a search for love. Love and truth co-exist to enhance and build on each other. So that when you love truth, this, in turn, yields greater capacity for love.

Truth and courage go hand in hand for one to express love to the optimum level. Truth implies an absence of fear and a presence of love. Thus truth, in essence, is love. If untruth unites with courage, the result is brutality in ones actions. With sincerity, patience, love for truth, kindness, supported by courage, you can learn to recognize love in its many different forms, thus rendering you spiritually richer than ever before.

When you love life, doors of opportunities begin to open up. Expansion of consciousness begins on the inner, and this impacts your outer consciousness in the like manner. Inner growth leads to outer changes, but we have to match our actions with our inner growth for this to be of any practical value, which makes for a balanced, integrated, and ever evolving individual.

When your life is guided by love, miracles follow. Love ensures that there is a continual outflow of Divine Spirit in your life as a daily practical reality. Life becomes filled with joy, love, adventure, and beauty. These elements co-exist to confirm the salubrious impact of the power of God. Your life and that of the presence of Divine Spirit become inseparable. Thus infuses your life with vibrancy and increased liveliness. However, this does not mean your life will be devoid of challenges or adversities. Challenges or adversities should not be looked at negatively. They are a part of the cosmic plan to raise us to new heights in our growth process. Therefore, they are blessings in disguise.

Living in obedience to God's will, one cannot fail because the active presence of God engenders the expansion of one's life. And to ensure this remains so, one must live from the heart and unfailingly lean upon the support of the infallible Divine Spirit within. With love like this, life becomes worth living.

The value of love is not in its abstraction but indeed in your actions. Watch how you give of yourself to others, putting yourself in their shoes to better understand their needs. Such understanding will change how you relate to others and how you serve them. Be careful with what secret thoughts you hold in your mind. Keep your thoughts clean, for they may manifest into your outer reality. Negative or positive thoughts may impact your life accordingly, depending on what thoughts you harbor habitually.

It helps to remember that love should not be locked within your human consciousness. You must manifest it, pass it on.

&

For it to be of any value, you must demonstrate it to those you love. You must make it a reality, for that is what God intends for you.

Giving love to others is not always as easy it sounds. One can easily fall into the trap of being a people pleaser and mistake it for love. Love is universal, therefore comes in different ways and forms relative to each situation. Loving another could be as simple as showing respect for another person. As it is not limited to just people and animals, it could also be love for truth, a hobby, an interest, a job, practically anything. It can also come in our conduct to instill discipline. Hence being firm does not always come from the position of power, but sometimes truly from love. It can also be gentle, too, when there is a natural flow of mutual trust, understanding, and respect.

If we were to give without expecting anything in return, life would reward us a hundredfold. If we were to give without placing conditions on the person we are giving; life would repay us either through the person we gave the gift or through another way unrecognizable by our limited human mind. Life always gives us back in some way, if not sooner, then later. That is why a person who always gives when needed and when able, always receives blessings from life abundantly. For in giving, there is a power beyond measure.

Common goals, interests cannot be emphasized enough. They are unifying points in a relationship. The more you have in common, the better, the stronger, the happier, the longer-lasting and more fulfilling your relationship will be. If you have no common points of interest, you will end up with a relationship with divergent interests, thus a lot of areas in which less reason to support and appreciate the value of another. One will tend not to value the other out of the perceived notion that what one is involved in is of little or no importance, automatically leading one to be judgmental. That already becomes a recipe for potential discontent in a relationship. Two people will soon grow apart. The magic power of love soon dies.

ℭ

When there is constant discord between two people that love each other, love begins to wane, the end of a relationship becomes an inevitability sooner or later.

So, follow your heart, be sincere, be patient, be understanding, give room for another to make errors and room to correct themselves. Be forgiving of yourself and your mate, do not be judgmental, allow your mate to be right even when you believe you are right. Be loving above all else. It's rewarding beyond words to find someone with whom to share genuine love.

If we were to render help when not needed,
we may be inadvertently taking away
someone's needed lesson or experience,
which would do a disservice to that person.
The person may need to go through that
situation for them to learn a much needed
spiritual lesson in their life. With the
lesson learned, one grows spiritually.

The gifts from God serve a dual purpose; One, to enrich our personal lives, Two, to improve and uplift society. In other words, gifts from God are not selfish gifts. They are selfless and universal because all things made out of God's material are selfless. By receiving these gifts and using them, we bring more light into our lives and in others' lives.

When they say God loves you, it's you as Soul, this reference is made to, irrespective of whether you are considered bad or good, and regardless of your religion. It's Soul that God is interested in, and its survival, growth and maturity. It's God's child, you, He wishes to return to its throne as a loving child of God.

When God works actively through you, He will guide you to His home. He will open your eyes to His actions. He will free you from the shackles of this world. And once freed, you will soar to greater spiritual heights. In fine, you must love to have your spiritual life fulfilled. Fulfilled in the spiritual sense, yet all aspects of your life will also get enriched in the process. And that is the far-reaching influence of God once allowed to be an active part of your daily life.

When God enters your life at a deeper level, it affects how you love others. The greater this depth is, the higher your love for others. So, allowing God to enter your life in a committed way without dictating to Him, expands your heart's capacity for Divine Love and ability to pass it on to the universe where it truly belongs.

Without love, you cannot move forward in your spiritual journey. Without love, you cannot build on anything with any measure of meaning and longevity, spiritually. It's only God's love that creates and supports life even though people are not always aware of it. Without an element of love for anything, nothing lasts for long. Because God builds and sustains through love. It's the only stuff that assures an upward ascent to higher, glorious spiritual heights.

To love God is to build life. So always strive to do things that are positive, truthful, and uplifting, and life will repay you well.

જી

Learn to love God because, with that, your life will change for the better. A life guided by God's love, filled with love, founded on love, is indeed a blessed life.

When you love a dog, it's God's creation, you are loving – the Soul of a dog. The outer aspect is the manifestation of God as a byproduct – a vital element of an extension of the inhabitant – Soul. This love is that which transcends the outer appearance. It connects Soul to Soul in a way that eludes human understanding. It is that which honors the divinity of another Soul.

When you realize love is an aspect of all living things, your attitude toward life changes. With this new attitude, you will begin to recognize that every experience has a spiritual dimension to it. Your respect for life heightens. You gain insight and realize that all life experiences happen for your benefit, therefore designed to serve you and move you closer to God. Life is no longer what you've always viewed it to be; you come to realize that there is more to life than that seen with the outer eye. You discover that life is now an integrated manifestation of the play of God.

ख

To live life with a loving attitude is to embrace life without fear, for one knows that God exists in all things. This awareness itself should instill a higher love for life. And your relationship with life will become that of respect and love for all life in whatever form it presents itself. Thus partaking in life is equivalent to participating in God's daily presence. Because God is everywhere and in everything around us, so are His blessings.

About the Author

Eric Chifunda is a New York–based occupational therapist who works as an independent contractor licensed in New York and New Jersey.

Awarded Editor's Choice Award in 2006 by poetry.com and the International Library of Poetry.

He is also an actor and an artist who intertwines visionary, abstract, and representational forms geared toward opening people's hearts.

www.ingramcontent.com/pod-product-compliance
Lightning Source LLC
Chambersburg PA
CBHW051203120626
46547CB00012B/1185